And So It Goes

A Companion to "Letters to Betty"

Mary Bub

GREEN HEART
LIVING
— PRESS —

DEDICATION

This book is dedicated

to all of those who walk the grief journey

with others authentically,

with patience and gentle guidance.

And for

Carolyn and Caryn

CONTENTS

Introduction

Writing to Betty was a difficult and surprising journey. It was not one that I had planned or that I had thought much about. Then, in the middle of a process that we can name the grief and loss journey, it came to me that there may be others who could benefit from the lessons, awareness, and understanding that grace was giving me. After the publication of *Letters to Betty*, I was offered an invitation to write a companion piece that might help others understand better the process that was now on the printed page.

What exactly is a process? *Dictionary.com* tells us that process is "a series of actions that produce a change or development; a method of doing or producing something; a forward movement; the course of time."

For me the action was my discipline and intention to write to Betty each day. I hoped to find a forward movement, a lessening of my grief, an understanding of my feelings in the course of time.

Now, I begin by sharing with you my reason for choosing the title for the book.

"And so it goes" was one of my mom's favorite things to say when she thought that there was nothing else to add or say. I chose it as the title of this companion to *Letters to Betty* because I found that there was more to say. There was a need to explain some of the ideas for healing and well-being found in the Letters.

Companion: "Someone who travels with you or spends time with you. A person or thing that enhances or supports your journey." (Merriam-Webster)

This description is one that I hope will hold true as an aid to one's grief or loss journey. Who doesn't like to have a companion along for the ride? The companion that you are holding in your hands is the result. I sincerely hope that it brings you not only an understanding of my journey but yours as well.

As I meet with small groups longing for peace, calm, and a way to process their own journeys, I hope that this companion becomes a welcome traveler.

I also feel that by dissecting my story into an outline of the concepts that I know can help another find understanding and hopefully healing, it can be an aid to the journey through any loss.

Together, we will:

- Identify words that can help describe the journey through grief or another kind of loss.

- Introduce various ways to process or find a vehicle to carry your personal story.

- Learn about a formula that is helpful in navigating the journey.

- Explore the reasons that symbols, metaphors, and language can make the narrative come alive.

- Begin to sketch out one's personal story and its relevance to the grief journey.

- Come to some understanding of our personal experience of grief or loss.

A Companion's Tale

Don't walk behind me
I may not lead
Don't walk in front of me
I may not follow
Just walk beside me
And be my friend.

Anonymous

What Good Then Is Our Grief?

What might we think or say of our time of mourning?

Do we hold it close without any thought to others?

How might we find goodness or mercy in this time of
grief or any loss for that matter?

No one can assign a path forward.

Each one must traverse the journey in their own time.

There can be solace however in finding a companion, a
person, or place or thing that is always present to our
need.

A companion who holds our truth, our story gently
with deep respect and honor.

Would that you will find your companion and that
your grief will find its way to a peaceful heart.

Would that you might see yourself as that companion
for another.

PART ONE
THE BEGINNING

No one wakes up one day and says, "I can't wait until I am into the grief, mourning, or bereavement process." Here in the middle of my own process, I realize that we are in this process during the whole of our lives. Being born into life in itself suggests that we have entered a journey. Born into something, the beginning of something, we soon come to learn that the something is our life story. (Letters to Betty, page 7.)

There is no simple way to describe what happens when grief or loss comes knocking on your door. Facing grief, I knew I had to make a beginning; a start at my new reality. I was efficient. It has always been one of the roles I played in my life and in my family. When all of the tasks were accomplished, however, I was numb and in shock. I asked myself: *Where do I go from here? Where will I find purpose now?* Having always been independent, I now find that too many days I wish that the person I found to be dependent on me was gone.

We experience the death of members of our families, our friends, our community. And we grieve. How might we walk through this end–of–life process openly, authentically, and with grace? I really didn't know.

Two things were important for me: sharing my thoughts and emotions truthfully, and finding purpose and meaning in the process.

It seemed as though I was a long way from feeling that I would find purpose in my every day now that my calendar was empty. The past few years had been filled with a plethora of appointments for Don. I was the keeper of the calendar and he would often refer to me as such.

As I stepped back into a time of solitude to ponder these questions, I realized that words have always been important to me. I am not a person who has ever been able to do journaling on a regular basis. Still, I have enjoyed writing short essays, newsletter articles, and short stories. I thought maybe that was the answer. Maybe I could let go of what I didn't do and step into a new way of using my words. I really enjoy getting notes, cards and letters from my friends. What if I wrote letters?

I began the letter writing and soon realized that they were not only for me. I clearly believed that what I was experiencing could be shared and perhaps even be helpful to others traveling the same path. This intention stayed with me and is still in my heart and soul. (See "A Hundred Black Birds" *Letter to Betty,* page 237.)

I might say that I was feeling like I was in the middle of a very rainy season. What, like the blackbirds, will I share of the feast after the storm?

Part Two
Every Journey Needs a Map

Without words or story in our lives, there is meaningless blank space.

Words become a part of the map of every journey I go on. I enjoy words, even when it is challenging to find just the right ones. I find words help guide me through the vast landscape of my emotions and random thoughts.

> *"Born into something, the beginning of something, we come to learn that the something is our life story." (Letters to Betty, page 7.)*

You will soon realize that story is a mainstay of my understanding of this current journey—the one that I might call my grief journey. It could even be called my grief story. We can be aware that the words used to describe the journey and the story bring us to meaning. In our lives, we encounter events that bring us great joy, great longing, great expectations, and grief and loss. Without words, there cannot be a story.

What exactly is the definition of grief? I asked myself.

> *"Grief is the emotional response to loss, such as the death of a loved one, a divorce, or a serious illness, aging, or leaving a home. It can also be a reaction to the loss of a pet, a job, or a dream. It is a process that includes multiple emotions." – Dr. Robert Niemeyer*

There is no right or wrong answer to the question, "what does grief feel like?" No two people feel grief or loss in exactly the same way and still after a time there can be an understanding of individual emotions.

And so, what does grief feel like? Sadness, Anger, Anxiety, Fear, Numbness, Shock, Guilt.

And so it goes, and even Gratitude and Happiness.

(See feeling word list in appendix.)

Now, we have words that might or might not enrich our story. Each person's story is unique to their own life experiences and the many events that create their personal storyline. Thus, each person's word lists are their own. Aaron Zerah in his book *As You Grieve: Consoling Words from Around the World,* tells us, "We seek peace from sources that offer consolation. We look for words that can touch our pain and show us that healing is indeed in store for us."

Through the process of writing *Letters to Betty*, I realized that my vocabulary had become very small. It was in the letter writing that I discovered that I had a much greater lexicon than I had imagined. Words came to me, and I was grateful for them because they helped me embrace what I was feeling and they became part of my grief journey. One of the new words I discovered still comes to me from time to time: morbs.

Morbs means, "Temporary melancholia. Coined from the adjective morbid."[1] The British lexicographer Susie Dent describes "having the morbs" as "to sit under a cloud of despondency."[2]

As we continue to walk with our companion, I am more and more confident that these gifts of words will be helpful to others.

Stories show us what it is like to be human, sometimes showing us the heights of the human spirit in overcoming adversity. Stories can help us identify our thoughts and emotions as we relate to the characters in the story. At times the characters in our story can say out loud what we can only identify in our hearts.

Prompts for Reflection or Group Sharing

---

1. According to the book *Passing English of the Victorian Era* (1909) by James Redding Ware.

2. https://en.wikipedia.org/wiki/Got_the_morbs

- How would you complete the sentence, "Grief is..." OR... "Grief feels like..."

- How important do you think developing a process that includes story and words that may be out of the norm for you can be helpful?

- Do you think that sharing your own journey can be helpful to others?

- How have you been enriched by listening to someone else's story?

Wisdom

Thinking of yourself as a character in a story is helpful when trying to identify your feelings in a particular situation. Sharing your story with a trusted friend clarifies your own character and might be helpful to them as well.

The Seven Whispers

1. *Maintain peace of mind*

2. *Move at the pace of guidance*

3. *Surrender to surprise*

4. *Ask for what you need*

5. *Offer what you can*

6. *Love the folks in front of you*

7. *Return to the World*

-Christina Baldwin, The Seven Whispers: A Spiritual Practice for Times Like These[3]

---

3. https://christinabaldwin.com/books/the-seven-whispers/

PART THREE
MEET BETTY

*"Story is the song line of a person's life. We
need to sing it and we need someone to hear
it. Story told, story heard, story written,
story read create the web of life in words."
(Christina Baldwin, Storycatcher: Making
Sense of Our Lives through the Power and
Practice of Story)*

I believe that stories can become the vehicle that carries
the narrative. The song line. While traveling my own
journey I found this to be true. But, who will I trust to
hear my story and understand why I need to share it? The answer to this question became Betty.

There was a song that was popular when my girls
were young. The gist of it was about being there for
one another, having each other's backs. We would sing
the song from time to time when a single hug was
necessary. I decided that Betty was just the right person

to receive my heartfelt letters. My imaginary friend, Betty, helped me find the right process through which I could express myself without judgment or critique.

Even though Betty is an imaginary recipient, I still felt that she heard me and understood what I was trying to say. The whole idea of addressing my grief process journey through letter writing felt comfortable. It was just between Betty and me. At times I would have enjoyed her being a real person who could and would answer my questions. Still, putting them down on paper helped me see them for what they were and they were so helpful to my coming to grips with my thoughts and feelings.

Letter Writing as Process

- When was the last time you wrote a letter?

- If you were to write a letter today, who would you be writing it to?

- How do you feel about the idea of processing your story in this way?

(See the appendix for a handout about letter writing to form connections. Writing to process one's own thoughts and feelings is personal and can be shared or not.)

Suggested Activity

Take paper and pencil or your keyboard and choose to grace an imaginary recipient with a letter.

1. What are you feeling right now?

2. What are you thinking about?

3. Can you find a metaphor to help you describe your thoughts and feelings today?

Wisdom

There are always more words in the universe than can ever be used so don't be afraid to use them or search for them. They are your truth, the foundation of your emotional intelligence. They can make you happy and they can help you heal from the trauma of grief and loss. It doesn't matter what others think about you having an imaginary recipient for your letters or your story sharing.

Find your Betty or your real-life friend and let your story become the vehicle that holds you in healing and loving arms.

"There comes a day
when you realize turning the page is the best feeling in
     the world,
because you realize
there's so much more to the book
than the page you were stuck on."
–Zayn Malik

PART FOUR

HELP FOR NAVIGATING THE JOURNEY

Searching for new methods to navigate your journey can be valuable. Reaching back into what has helped you reach your destination in the past may just be an easier road to take.

A formula that has seen me through my work as a facilitator of process-oriented circles of women has become a stalwart for me. It is one that I learned from a wise woman who taught me much about finding my way through various experiences in my life.

When I thought about writing this companion, I immediately reached into my tried-and-true book of formulas and patterns. I am using my favorite here. They are Experience, Remembrance, Choices, and Filling the Void. I am confident that they will help us navigate our current journeys.

There is another thing that we will encounter on our journey. I call it the grief box.

The grief box is an imaginary box that resides in my head. In it are stored all of the emotions and maybe even some thoughts about my grief and its journey. The grief journey is one that insists on all of a person being present. At times it is hard for me to get out of my head and reintroduce myself to my feelings. The grief box was the gift that was just what I needed. Eventually, it became, along with Betty, another character in the story and a companion on the journey.

The grief box almost fell off the shelf today. When this happens, everything comes spilling out. It is usually not a great day when this happens. Instead, I started to think about which pieces I did not need any longer. Just where am I in the process everyone calls "grief? Still sad and lonely, I find myself remarkable feeling grateful. I think my fractured pieces are starting to be put back together. (Letters to Betty, page 15.)

PART FIVE
EXPERIENCE THEN AND NOW

No one wakes up one day and says, "I can't wait until I am into the grief, mourning, or bereavement process." Here in the middle of my own process I realize that we are in this process during the whole of our lives. Being born into life in itself suggests that we have entered a journey. (Letters to Betty, page 7.)

How might we walk through this end-of-life process openly, authentically, and with grace? Perhaps by taking the time to learn about our past experiences of grief and loss. How we face death or loss, how we cope, and how we heal, are affected by the messages and values that were learned in the earlier chapters of our life story. Our emotional maturity is shaken when we encounter raw and painful grief or loss.

I was a come-late-in-life child. My sisters were 11 and 13 years older than me. Therefore, my relatives were also much older than I was. Some of my most vivid memories are attending funerals for family members, friends, and neighbors. As I grew into adulthood, helping to arrange these events became part of my responsibility. I remember well a time when my dad, who is long gone now, took me aside and told me that I had done a good job. Although there are many other things I would have been happy to hear from him, I took it as high praise.

Suggested Activity

Introduce Sally Story - Stories awaken life's learning and yearning. Sally is a symbol for personal story.

> *Symbol – "Something real that stands for or suggests another thing that cannot in itself be pictured or shown." (Merriam–Webster)*

(Sally is a small white teddy bear that lives in a glittery bag. Any symbol with the correct letters would do or perhaps a poster as well.) What are some of the stories that have brought you learning? For example: family lore, mistakes, or misdemeanors.

Are there stories that cause you to yearn for what has been lost? For example: relationships, shared experiences, personality quirks.

Metaphor: "A figure of speech in which a word or phrase meaning one kind of object or idea is used in place of another to suggest a similarity between them." (Merriam-Webster)

Prompts for Reflection or Group Sharing

Grief is a roundabout. There are many options. If you miss your exit you just keep going around and around. Finally you choose an exit and leave the roundabout. Then the journey truly begins. (Letters to Betty, page 4.)

Name the possible exits on the roundabout. For example: Anxiety, confusion, sadness, loneliness, hope, new beginnings, healing, peace, create, gratitude.

Can you think of others?

Wisdom

Asking ourselves the how, when, and why of our reactions to these situations can be invaluable and can bring understanding.

- No two stories or journeys are completely alike; they may have similar characteristics, but they can only be owned by the one who has been in the experience.

- What were the stories or myths or beliefs that you heard that have informed your view of loss.

PART SIX
REMEMBRANCE

Memories, wonderful, needed, and fickle. I heard myself talking to the friend that I don't want to share with anyone else. She listens to me, questions me, supports me and together we work through deeper questions then, what do you think about climate change. What I noticed was I talked about Don and I didn't get emotional or even the least bit weepy. For days I couldn't let myself go to the place of any memory without crying. So, pulling out the stoic part of me I just stopped trying to remember anything. Memories can be wonderful. We need them and we can choose to allow them to be fickle or instead a source of deep comfort. Especially when they are shared. They make up much of our grief or loss story." (Letters to Betty, page 15.)

Memories are wonderful and fickle. Often when grieving one has little control over their memories.

They can give comfort if the memory is one that is kind.

They can be fickle when the memory reminds us of the times that were not so pleasant or in which we see ourselves in ways that bring us to regret or longing for what has been lost.

Wisdom

It is far better to remember and cry than to deny oneself the contents of learning that can be had from each and every memory. Isn't it how we are supposed to keep our loved ones with us? Aren't they supposed to reside somewhere in our soul or in the marrow of our bones?

Stay authentic.

Own all of your truth. What are all of the parts of the loss experience? Allow humanness.

Be storytellers and story catchers.

Share your stories when you are open and ready to do so.

Mind when others are asking for them or willing to hear them.

Listen to the stories of others and help them to catch the truth, understanding or message that they are giving.

"Story is our nearest
And dearest way of
Understanding our lives
And finding our way forward."
– Ursula LeGuin

PART SEVEN
CHOICES

The grief process is at times a long, difficult process and at others a blessing.

> *No one wakes up one day and says, "I can't wait until I am into the grief, mourning, or bereavement process." Here in the middle of my own process, I realize that we are in this process during the whole of our lives. (Letters to Betty, page 7.)*

Back to the roundabout. You have the resources within yourself to choose your own grief journey. You have the right to exit the roundabout when you choose. Another quote that I find to be true is from Ann Dawson in her book *A Season of Grief,* "Grief will release its grip on us only when all of our grief work is completed. This may take a week, a year, or the rest of our lives. It's only when we accept our state of grief and lean into it, embrace it as part of our being, that the pain will begin to ease."

I chose this quote because it amplifies again the metaphor of "journey" and the idea of a grief story. I included it here because I believe it is important to our companion. It tells us again that our journey may be a bumpy road, under construction even, but we can decide when we reach acceptance and when we are ready to exit the roundabout. Perhaps, one of the exits is titled patience. Maybe one can return to the roundabout at various times in their personal grief story and add another chapter.

(See "Ordinary Things", *Letters to Betty*, page 11.)

The practice of ordinary things can be applied not only to grief and loss but to anxiety and stress as well. It is grounding, asks nothing of you, except something healing and familiar.

Learning this practice was and is a grace and a blessing.

It takes a companion, someone you trust to hold your story in gentle hands, offering support without judgment.

The roundabout is yours, however the community that is yours can be most helpful when they call you to the next step in your journey outside of the roundabout.

> *"It may be that when we no longer know what to do, we have come to do our real work. And when we no longer know which*

way to go, we have begun our real journey."
- Wendell Berry

You may find that your friends or community have changed.

At times, others do not know how to respond to your needs.

What was may not be what you need now.

Part of embracing this new journey, this new chapter in your story, may be engaging with a different companions or community. Or, creating one for yourself.

Wisdom

Take a moment or a day and think about the friends you have cherished, the ones who are always there for you. Consider who you might invite into your circle to help you process your experience of grief and loss. Choose wisely, choose those who hold you gently in their honest embrace. Choose those who are there with you for the long haul, quietly, intentionally and for as long as it takes.

Part Eight

Filling the Void with Action

Only in being willing to accept the emptiness can we begin to fill it.

Loss leaves us empty.

Loss leaves us empty, without our context, lacking understanding, living in a blank space.

Use the word list, choose all of those that describe your inner wellbeing at the time of the loss.

How do we fill the void?

Take your time, listen to your inner voice, and find a process that works for you. (Write a letter, journal, support group, regular phone call with a trusted friend, or prayer. Remember which exit you decided to take off of the roundabout and continue to act on it.)

Form an intention (ordinary things). Write it down and refer to it often.

Reach out for help or reach in to give help.

Whether you are a socially motivated person who needs input from others, or you are inclined to quietly unpack your own thoughts and feelings, you have the resources to fill the void.

Wisdom

"There comes a day when you realize turning the page is the best feeling in the world, because you realize there's so much more to the book than the page you were stuck on." - Zayn Malik

"Today is life-the only life you are sure of. Make the most of today. Get interested in something. Shake yourself awake. Let the winds of enthusiasm sweep through you. Live today with gusto." - Dale Carnegie

"What you do makes a difference, and you have to decide what kind of difference you want to make." - Jane Goodall

APPENDIX

Feelings Word List

sad	desolation	annoyance
lost	despondency	discomfort
empty	dejection	aggravation
alone	despair	vexation
melancholy	angst	indignation
depressed	mortification	trouble
numb	mourning	distress
sorrow	mournfulness	agitation
misery	bereavement	bother
sadness	lamentation	irritability
anguish	lament	outrage
pain	remorse	upset
distress	regret	resentment
agony	pining	disturbance
torment	blues	pique
affliction	dolor	umbrage
suffering	dole	ire
heartache	frustration	angriness
heartbreak	exasperation	dudgeon
broken-heartedness	irritation	snappishness
heaviness of heart	anger	gall
woe	displeasure	dander

Letter Writing Handout

Letter writing can be helpful in any process.

When practicing letter writing or, rather, using letter writing as part of your inner journey practice you may find that you feel a sense of accomplishment. You might, I hope, also find comfort in the fact that you are able to put words to your feelings in a way that you could decide to share with a trusted friend. Or two or three maybe.

Should you decide to actually purchase some lovely stationery and pen a letter to someone, I know that you will be experiencing purpose in providing a surprise of caring to the recipient.

You may experience a sense of success, the building of human connections, an opening of your mind and heart, giving you greater perspective. You could even find that letter writing eases feelings of loneliness and isolation.

Afterword

If I could have one wish, one hope about this companion, it would be that whoever uses it whether personally or with others, might find both understanding and some peace of mind.

It has been my pleasure and my honor to travel this journey and now it is time for me to take the exit marked: What now? Who now? Where now? And so it goes.

With very much gratitude,

Mary Bub

About the Author

Mary Bub is a grassroots activist and social innovator. She is the co-founder, past president and currently an advisor of Wisconsin Rural Women's Initiative, www.rural women's initiative.org, a nonprofit organization that provides on-site grassroots programs to individual women and organizations through a Gathering Circle process promoting personal development, transformation and systemic change. She is the winner of the Social Innovation Prize in Wisconsin for 2008, A Purpose Prize Fellow with Civic Ventures, recipient of the Feminarian Award and winner of Wisconsin's Top Rural Development Initiatives.

Mary is a widow, mother, grandmother, great grandmother, friend, facilitator of a small circle of Kindreds and Officiant of Memorial Services. She lives on MoonStar Farm with her dog York and cat Liza.